ADVERTISEMENT.

In consequence of the solicitations of his friends, the Author has at length decided on publishing the History of his Life. As he has aimed at brevity, he has only recorded those circumstances which were the most prominent, and which were most connected with his conversion. To give a view of the errors and superstitions in which he was educated, he has found it necessary to notice some of the Jewish Customs, but in doing this he has mourned over the bondage of his brethren, and prayed for their deliverance; and he trusts these parts of his little work will excite gratitude in the hearts of his Christian readers that they are favoured with the glorious light of Gospel truth. That the book may go forth with the blessing of God, and be useful to all, whether Jews or Gentiles, that may honour it with a perusal, is the ardent prayer of

THE AUTHOR.

January, 1833.

HISTORY AND CONVERSION.

***

When I reflect how long I trod
The crowded path which leads from God,
  The God who gave me breath;
I stand amaz'd that love divine,
Should rescue this poor soul of mine,
  From everlasting Death.

***

WHEN I meditate on my origin, that " I am but dust and ashes," that in sin my mother conceived me, and that I was shapen in iniquity; when I think that I was born of that race of men, who, times without number, have provoked the Holy One to anger—of that race who have killed the Prince of Life, and desired a murderer to be granted in his place, my soul is ready to exclaim, " What am I, and what is my father's house, that I should be visited so kindly." God has spared my life by mercy, which is beyond expression. I walked for the space of eighteen years in the ways of Judaism,—ways in which neither the loud voice of the warning trumpet that sounded on Sinai, nor the awful thunders and lightnings that accompanied it, could keep my feet from falling. At any time when the ear caught the sound of thunder, or the eye perceived a flash of lightning, I, with the Jews, cried

A 3

out, "*Naaseh Vinishmo*," that is, "we will do, and be obedient;"* but no sooner did the thunder subside, and the lightning cease, than I, like the ancient Israel-ites, made a "Golden Calf," or like a dog to his vomit, I returned to my folly. But God being merciful to me, at length brought me forth from the house of bondage, and set my feet upon a sure rock, even the Rock Christ Jesus. And has he done so much for me? Has he brought me out of the mire and clay? Has he snatch-ed me as a brand from the burning? And shall I ever forget the day?

> "Since thou hast drawn my heart to thee,
> " Which was so hard and blind;
> " Oh! shall I cease to name, in praise,
> " Those years thou hast been kind?
> " O no, my Saviour! I'll thy love record,
> " And through my life confess thee only Lord."

Yes, and though I hope I am pressing forward to the mark of my high calling, yet will I not forget those things that are behind; but I will look back to the hole of the pit whence I was digged, and I will declare to all them that fear thee, what thou hast done for my soul.

In the year 1807, I was born in Warsaw, the capi-tal of Poland. My parents were Jews, and as far as I can trace back, they were regularly descended from Jews; and though not of the sect of the Pharisees, yet they paid all their own, and thanked God they

---

* Whenever it thunders and lightens rather out of the common way, the Jews open the Bible with the ten commandments before them, and stand at the window, calling to mind the promise they made when they received them, viz. *Naaseh Vinishmo*, we will do, and be obedient.

were not extortioners, nor unjust persons, nor as bad as their neighbours. They fasted, and gave alms, and had a great regard for the law of God, as it was given by Moses. According to the Jewish custom I was therefore circumcised on the eighth day, and the other Mosaical laws and Rabbinical ceremonies (which are six hundred and thirteen in number,) were taught me as fast as my infant mind could embrace them. When I was three years old, I was able to use the " *Tsitsith*,"* mentioned in the fifteenth chapter of Numbers, from the 37th to the 47th verse, and could repeat the prayers appointed to them by our Rabbies, which are thirteen verses selected from the law of Moses, in commemoration of the Israelites coming out of Egypt. And here I would observe, that although it was a ceremonial law and religion my parents taught me, yet I hope I shall never forget to be thankful to them, or cease to pray

* The *Tsitsith* is sometimes called *Arba Canphoth* from having four corners, it is a kind of vestment, which is worn constantly as an inner garment, and consists of two quadrangular pieces of cloth, either of linen, silk, or woollen, joined together at the upper edge by two broad straps, with a space left sufficient for the head to pass between them. These straps rest on the shoulders, and the two square pieces hang down, one over the back, and the other over the breast, from each of the corners hangs a fringe, the threads composing the fringes are of wool that has been shorn, and spun by the hand of a Jewess for this purpose. Four of these threads are passed through a small hole made about the breadth of three fingers from each edge, forming the angle:—These threads are to be doubled to make eight; seven are equal in length, and the eighth must be long enough to bind the other seven together five distinct times, and afterwards to have an end of the same length as the other seven. These fringes they kiss repeatedly every morning at their prayers. The Rabbies teach that those who neglect the use of the *tsitsith* are exceedingly wicked.

for them, for it was the law of Moses that convinced me of the truth as it is in Jesus.

I was about four years old when I commenced going to an Hebrew school, where I learned to read and write the holy tongue, as the Jews call it. There I was distinguished by my schoolmaster as being very quick of comprehension, and he ventured to foretel to my sanguine relations that I should become, at a time not far distant, a noted rabbi in Israel. He paid great attention to me, and I was soon able to read not only in the books of Moses, but also the Talmudical writings, to the great satisfaction of those who were not aware of my private conduct, but to my father and mother who have often listened with astonishment to various questions I proposed on some of the rabbinical writings, it was often disheartening. They were afraid I should become an "*Apicoureth,*" that is, a ridiculer of God's word, or an infidel. The following is a specimen of some of the questions I asked my father, and for which he pronounced me an "*Apicoureth.*"

Coming home one day from school, my father (as is the custom among Jews,) asked me " what I had learned that day ?" "I learned to-day, and Jacob went out from Beer-sheba, meaning the 28th chapter of Genesis, from the 10th verse." " Have you learned it with Rashai?"* " Yes, father," I replied, "and I know all about the stones in the 18th verse." " What question does Rashai ask there, and what does he answer?" "He asks the reason why it is written in the 18th

* The name of the most noted Jewish commentator.

verse, and Jacob rose up early in the morning, and took *the stone* that he had for his pillow, yet in the second verse it appears he had *many* stones for a pillow." "Well done," said my father, "and what answer does he make?" "Why, it is funny: he says when Jacob laid down, the stones, began to make a noise. One of them said, on me this holy man shall lay his head; and the others said, nay, but on me he shall lay his head: so that there was a great quarrel among them, and Jacob could not sleep: then the Almighty made out of all the stones, *one* stone, and when Jacob got up in the morning he took "the stone," for they all became one. Now, do you think, father, that Rashai was there, and heard when the stones made a noise and quarrelled?" My father gave me a slap on the cheek, and said I was an "*Apicoureth.*"

At another time, on coming from the school, he asked me to tell him something about *Birishith*, meaning the first of Genesis. I told him, with other things, Rashai's question and answer on the sixteenth verse. Rashai says it is written in the latter part of this verse, that the greater light was to rule the day, and the lesser light to rule the night, and yet it seems from the first part of the verse, that they were both created great lights. How comes the lesser one? He answers thus—God, in fact, created the lights with equal lustre, but the moon was dissatisfied, and said to her Maker, it does not look well for two noblemen to be of one degree, when they are each above serving one another, it would be far better if one of us were inferior. This was hinting that the sun had better be lessened; but God, for the impudence of the moon, commanded her to be the *lesser* one: but seeing the moon in despondency, God granted stars for her assistance. "Now," I said to my father, " I am sure Rashai did not hear this conversation, as there was no man created then." My father, as before, called me an "*Apicoureth.*" My parents, however, persevered in giving me every necessary instruction. My mother often observed, "he is but a child, he will be wiser as he gets older." My father became of the same opinion, and bore with me. But my mother loved me.

I was now about six years of age, and I was committed to a higher school, to improve in the Talmud, and it would be impossible for me to relate the pains my dear parents took with me between this and the time I was twelve years of age. I cannot but feel grateful to them when I consider the prayers they took care I should say every morning and evening, the tales they told me of good children, that I might follow their example, and the high opinion they gave me of the Creator of the universe, by telling me of his greatness, that I might adore him; of his power, that I might fear him; of his goodness, that I might trust in him; and of his love, that I might admire him. Yea, so constant were their endeavours to " train me in the way in which they thought I should go," that I believe they were of opinion, that in this way I should find my peace flowing as a river, and my righteousness as the waves of the sea;" but in this, alas! they were disappointed, for not only is the law of Moses a yoke, that neither our fathers nor we were able to bear, but I was also naturally inclined to evil; for in spite of their endeavours, the instruction of my teachers, and advice of my friends and well-wishers, I followed the evil inclinations of my own heart, "rejoicing in my youth, walking in the sight of mine own eyes, and did not consider that for all these things God would bring me into judgment." But did God allow me to go on in this way without checking me? O, no! to my shame I must confess, that often I heard the voice of the Lord God in my soul, and I feared, and would have hid myself from his presence, had I known where. But whither can a sinner go from his spirit? or whither shall he fly from his presence? If he ascends up into heaven, he is there; if he makes his bed in hell, behold there he is; let him take the wings of the morning and fly to the uttermost parts of the sea, even there is his hand, and his right hand shall hold him fast; yea, the darkness hideth not from him, for the darkness and the light are both alike to him." Sometimes when I had well drunk of the cup of folly and sin, I did not regard the advice of my friends, nor listen to the voice of conscience, (for Jews have a conscience as well as Christians,) God laid his hand of affliction upon me, and that in various ways. Once I was near being drowned when bathing, without my mother's knowledge; and once, instead of going to school, I was watching a joiner driving a peg of wood into the ground, when, not perceiving me behind him, upon lifting the axe to prepare for another stroke, he hit me on my forehead, and it was through the mercy of God that 1 was not killed on the spot. Besides these, 1 had many other accidents and lingering sicknesses; and in some of these instances 1 did bend to the chastening hand of God, as my dear mother always took great care to remind me, that God was thus chastising me for my sins.* But these impressions were but of short duration; for having got saved from the water, cured of the wound made by the axe, and restored to health from sickness, 1 returned to my follies like a moth to the candle, where but a minute before its legs were burned. Thus, neither God's mercies, nor his judgments, nor the advice of my friends, induced me to follow the light 1 had. But what doth God say to this? " 1f ye will not for all this hearken unto me, but walk contrary unto me, then will 1 walk contrary unto you also in fury; and 1, even 1, will chastise you seven times for your sins." The Lord, however, corrected me, with judgment, not in his anger, lest 1 should be brought to nothing.

During the whole of this period of my life, 1 had

* I had neglected many times to wash before meat, had carried my "tsitsith" when they were imperfect, and had often neglected to use them. I was also conscious, of having used the knife intended for meat, to take butter, of having touched candlesticks on the Sabbath Days, and sometimes, did not attend to the rabbinical laws as regards the cutting of my finger nails, and many other sins of this nature. These laws require the Jews to mind particularly which of the nails are cut first, and which last, and after they are cut they are to put them carefully into a paper, with two or three chips cut off from the table legs or ends, as witnesses, and throw them into the fire.

not once heard of the name of Jesus Christ, as being the Messiah, and Saviour of the world; as the Jews, being such determined enemies to Christianity, use all means within their power to keep their children ignorant of its history and doctrines. There is the very same spirit among them now that there was in the Saviour's time. At that time they cried out " we will not have this man to reign over us," though they confessed "never man spoke like him." They cried out "away with him, crucify him," though his blood should be required at their, and their children's hands. The Jews still are wrapped in prejudice and determined to fight against him, without considering they may be found fighting against God. The Rabbies it seems were afraid lest the Jews would become enlightened, if they should either think, or talk of Christ; for this they very strictly prohibit, and the Jews scarcely ever mention the name of Christ, unless when they blaspheme him! Children are taught to abhor, not only the name, which is to the conscious sinner dear, but even men and places that are named by him. The schoolmasters forbid their scholars to look up when they pass by a Christian place of worship, and direct them to spit out, and repeat, "abhor it with abhorrence, dislike it with disgust, for it is accursed."* These words they also repeat when they meet a priest, who is easily known by his dress. The Jews are in the habit of naming every thing that appears in the shape of an idol, "*tolou*," (the crucified,) the name which they give to Christ, and when the Ca-

* Deut. vii. 26.

B

tholics walk in procession carrying their images, the Jews commonly say, " they carry the *tolou*," (cruci-fied,) and the younger part of the Jews, are so used to this expression, that whenever they hear any one re-mark, that the Christians believe in "*tolou*," they know no better, or understand no more, than that Christians believe in images. Thus they are kept in ignorance, and thus they will remain, till God shall in mercy in-terfere. I was now in my twelfth year, and was ignorant that there ever appeared one who claimed to be the Sa-viour of the world.

About this time, two Missionaries came to Warsaw from the London Society for promoting Christianity among the Jews. Having learned that they gave away books gratis, I ran to them and asked one of them to give me one of their books, I wished to have one of the pretty bound books, viz. a Testament, but he gave me a tract, and said, after he had spoken with me for a minute or two, if you will read this tract, and let me know what you have read when you come again, I will then give you one of these pretty books. I received the tract with joy, and the moment I came out of the house, I opened it and cast my eyes on the following words, or such like, "How long will the children of the house of Israel refuse to believe the truth as it is in Jesus Christ?" I was quite astonished, and I repeated in my mind; believe in Jesus the Mes-siah ! I never heard of him: who can this mean ? I could not read any further, but thought who Jesus was. While I was thus musing, I arrived at home, where I found my father just sitting down to dinner, and I ran up to him with a degree of pleasure, with the tract in my hand. "See, father," said I, "a gentleman gave me this as a present. Who is Jesus Christ it speaks about ?" I looked earnestly into his face, expecting to hear who Jesus was; but, oh! how can I express my sorrow to say that my dear father was so ignorant, and so much blinded with prejudice, that he tore and burned the tract in my sight, and after punishing me very severely, he ordered me to inquire no more after this name, on pain of being turned out of the house. I pleaded my ignorance, and told him I thought it was a good book, because it was written in the holy language : yet he would make no allowance for me, but repeated his threatenings. This appeared a very severe treatment to me then, but seeing now that was an instrument in the hands of the all-wise God, to bring me among the witnesses of the Saviour, I cannot help exclaiming with the Apostle, " How unsearchable are his judgments, and his ways past finding out !"

I concluded that my father did not punish me for inquiring after Jesus, but that he did not like me so well as my brothers and sisters, and therefore treated me badly in order to get me out of the house. I had not this long in my mind before I began to think of leaving home, and having heard of a gentleman that was in want of an errand-boy, I went and engaged myself to him, although in my father's house there was bread enough and to spare, even for hired servants. With this gentleman I lived about two years, during which period, I attempted several times to go home and see my mother, but my father never welcomed me, and sometimes ordered me out of the house, saying to my mother, "He will turn out a *Meshomet*, or an apostate, you'll see." Rather than be thus mortified by living in the vicinity of my relations, and not be permitted to see them, and by seeing my brothers and sisters idolized, and myself hated, I determined to beg my bread from door to door in a foreign land, where, if I should meet with bad usage, I should know it was from strangers. I said, summer is coming, I'll take out a passport, and leave my father's house, my kindred, and my native land, and go where God in mercy may direct me. These thoughts I soon put into action; and though my parents put obstacles in my way at first, yet when they found they could not hinder me, they consented. Leipsic fair was now approaching, and many merchants were setting out for it from Warsaw. I agreed with some of them to make their beds on the way,* and clean their shoes, and do any other thing they wished me to do, if they would let me ride in their waggon. The day for setting out having arrived, as is customary among the Jews, the waggon went about a mile out of the town, and the relations accompanied the travellers to take leave of them, and pronounce a blessing upon them. My mother walked with me, and gave me much good advice, and, as I stepped into the waggon, she said, go " *Bishem elohy yisroile,*" in the name of the God of Israel.

* It is common in Poland, for travellers to carry their beds with them

Having got quietly sat down in the waggon, I began to employ my leisure in meditating on my journey's end. A thousand difficulties appeared to me. I was aware I should soon have to leave the waggon, and what must I begin at then, said I, the twenty shillings that I have will soon be spent, and how shall I get to London, a distance of sixteen hundred miles? When I get there, to whom shall I go? for whom shall I inquire? I know nobody, and nobody knows me. When I want any thing, how shall I speak? I do not know a word of English. Such thoughts as these perplexed my mind for the first two or three days; but when the merchants engaged me to wait upon them at Leipsic, my mind became eased, and I hoped that Israel's God would help me yet. In ten days we performed our journey to Leipsic, and the merchants with whom I came, behaved kindly to me all the time they remained here, which was about three weeks. When they left the fair, they made me a present of a little money, so that I was able to keep up my twenty shillings. I now began to think of proceeding to Hamburgh, and sought for an opportunity, which I found with less trouble than I expected, as there was a waggoner there who had fled from the rigour of the Polish laws for selling contraband goods. He did not think himself safe even here, and determined to take his waggon to Hamburgh with passengers, and afterwards sell his waggon, and proceed to England. He promised to take me for nothing. At first I was greatly overjoyed, as I was in hopes of keeping my twenty shillings alive, by going along with him; but finding he was a desperate rogue, I feared lest the law would overtake him, and I should share in his punishment, though I had no share in his iniquity. I found out the day before our departure, that he intended to take away his waggon and horses from the inn by stealth, without paying what was due to the innkeeper for four weeks' rent for his apartments, and stabling and fodder for his horses, I trembled for myself, but I did not know what step to take to keep out of the mischief. On the afternoon before we went, he ordered me, in the presence of the innkeeper, to put the horses to the waggon and take it to the blacksmith, that he might examine the wheels, and then bring back the harness. I did so, and the next morning he again ordered me in the presence of the landlord, to take the horses and bring the waggon home. I obeyed, but while I was putting too the harness, he arrived, and said to me, "We can't do better than set off just now." I trembled like a fish as we were setting off. When we had proceeded about a mile out of the town, we arrived at a small water. He then put his hands into it, and lifting them and his eyes to heaven, begged God's mercy to enable him with safety to get through his adventure.*

Oh, foolish Jews! how can you expect God's blessing on your unjust doings? Well exclaims Moses—

---

* It would seem to me that he thought it no sin to take advantage of a Gentile, as Moses gave the Jews leave to lend them money on usury, while they were not allowed to take it of one another. Deut. xxiii. 20. But he forgot that it is also written, "Ye shall not add unto the word which I command you." Deut. iv. 2, and xii. 32.

" Do ye thus requite the Lord ?   O foolish people and unwise ; for all his ways are judgment ; a God of truth, and without iniquity : just and right is he."

As we were driving along, he repeatedly kept turning his head to see if he was pursued.   In fact, 1 believe that if his conscience had not been " seared with a red hot iron," he would have sunk under his fears ; for at the motion of a flying bird, at the shaking of the trees, at the movement of his own body, he shrunk and trembled, fancying in all these his pursuers were at hand, to " take him by the throat," saying, " pay me what thou owest."   Oh ! how true is that Scripture—" The way of transgressors is hard ; there is no peace to the wicked."

Nothing particular took place in our journey to Hamburgh, but being in constant fear, I was happy when we arrived there.   By the German Jews in Hamburgh, 1 was treated with kindness. One of them invited me to eat in his house the sabbatic feasts, which 1 did ; and he being astonished at my adventures, being, as he observed, but a child, he was induced to give me a little money, and recommend me to his friends, by whose assistance, though 1 stopped in Hamburgh a few days, 1 bore my expences without touching my twenty shillings.

On my fourth day in Hamburgh, 1 learned that there was a fine German brig, laden with the produce of the country, to sail for London, as soon as the wind answered her course, in which vessel fourteen Jewish passengers were shipped.   1 applied to the captain, told him 1 had no money, and would work my passage over. He smiled when 1 said 1 would work my passage, as he thought 1 was "fit for nothing." With the solicitations of the Jews in the brig, he consented to take me, on condition that 1 would find myself with provisions. 1 now went to buy them in, and my very heart sunk within me when 1 beheld my twenty shillings lessened to two and sixpence. 1 often mentioned my fears and griefs to the Jews on board, and they encouraged me by saying, "Be a good boy, and the God who fed Jacob from his youth, and blessed Ephraim and Manasseh, will not withhold his mercy from you."

The day we set sail from Hamburgh it was rather slack tide, and as we did not get out of the river before the tide was done, we were obliged to cast anchor, as we were heavy laden; meanwhile, a vessel homeward bound, and very lightly laden, was knocking about in the river, endeavouring to gain the port of Hamburgh against the wind. Either for want of caution, or some mismanagement, they ran against our vessel. We could not get out of their way, as we were fast at anchor, and it seems it was too late for them to prevent running against us, They broke our jibboom, and injured the bowsprit. While this was taking place, I perceived confusion in the face of the mariners, and the Jews, who had never witnessed such a scene in their lives before, thought it was all over with them, and began to cry out, "*Shemah yisroile*," Hear, O Israel, &c. However, as we got disentangled, we became more composed, and when all was over offered a thanksgiving, called by the Jews, "*Gomail Brochey*," viz. redeeming thanks. It took a day or two to get our damages repaired; and being equipped once more, we took advantage of the breeze and set sail.

The accommodations the Jews had on board were not of the best kind, as they had no separate births to sleep in, but were all together between decks, which the captain planked for their convenience, and put a kind of bulwarks fore and aft, to prevent their tumbling down the lower hold. They had a ladder to go up and down, fixed at the after hatch, a hole from which the cargo is lowered down into the ship's hold. In this place they laid out their bed-clothes for sleeping, and in the spare corners they set down their provisions, cooking utensils, &c. and they thought they had contrived all wonderfully, and with good taste: and so it appeared to them for the first two or three days when we had but little wind, and consequently little or no motion in the ship. But on the third night when it commenced 'blowing rather briskly, and the ship began a rocking something like a cradle, what a change took place in their minds! One cried out, "we should have put every thing in our chests, and the chests ought to have been screwed down." " Why did you not tell us this before," cried another, " for we might have saved all then?" Confusion now commenced. They and their utensils were rolling to and fro: some were screaming and howling, some cursing, and some praying, to the great rejoicing of the ship's crew, who seemed quite pleased as they peeped down the hold, and observed the general confusion. One woman cried out, "Read the second psalm." "Sammy," she cried to me, "read, why do the heathen rage," when an old man replied, "it is not the heathen that are raging, it is the fishes and the sea that make all this stir." Another woman said, "She had heard her father say, that throwing a spoonful of honey into the sea would calm the tempest. Would you (addressing herself to the old man who spoke before,) take my keg of honey, and throw a spoonful overboard, and see what it will do?" "Any thing to please you." So saying, he took the keg of honey and went on deck: returning in two or three minutes, he said, " Mother, one spoonful would do nothing, so I sent the whole keg overboard to see what it would do."

We now went on for some days without any particular occurrence, and though the weather was rough, nothing material happened either to the ship or company. During the whole of this time, I felt quite composed in my mind; but all on a sudden, hearing the Captain say " we shall be at Gravesend to morrow," melancholy seized me immediately. 1 awoke as it were out of my slumbers; and I thought what shall I do when I get there? what shall I begin at? to whom shall I make my wants known? oh, that the voyage would never end! But the wind was fair and brisk, and the next morning's sun disclosed the English shore; and in the early part of that afternoon, I found myself in the magnificent streets of London. The Captain to manifest his approbation of my conduct, made me a present of two shillings and sixpence, so that I had now five shillings to begin the world with, in the 14th year of my age.

I was then dressed in my own country fashion, which even in London appeared very singular, for hundreds of boys followed me as 1 passed to Duke's-Place, where the Jews are to be found. At present 1 do not wonder at it at all, and I think my readers will scarcely be able to refrain laughing when they think of my dress. A little boy about fourteen years of age, with a pair of German boots reaching up to the knees, with a large black tassel attached to each of the tops; add to this a pair of nankeen smallclothes, with a black silk waistcoat, and a lead coloured nankeen long coat, reaching down to the heels, without any laps or opening behind, and a hat on his head with a small crown, and a very broad rim, with a stick in one hand, and a bundle in the other. Here is the figure I made in the streets of London on my first arrival, with five shillings in my pocket, to seek my fortune. On the evening of that day, 1 found my way to the Jews, and very kindly they received me. The next day, they made up a collection for me among themselves, and put me in the way of laying in a stock, and of becoming a travelling dealer. Having tried for about a week in London this way of getting a living, and could do but very little, I determined to go into the country, and having laid out all my little money in goods, except a sixpence, which I preserved in case I should take no money soon, I set off from London towards Birmingham.

I need not say much on what I felt when I left London. This may be easily conceived, if my circumstances at that time be considered. I was a stranger in a strange land, scarcely knew a word of English, and had only sixpence in my pocket, with little prospect of taking any money that day : suffice it to say, I had a heavy heart, and an aching head.

I travelled the first day about twenty miles, and took no money, and having spent something during the day for refreshment, I had only twopence left. It was now near dark, and I did not know what to do for a lodging, as I was aware twopence would not pay for one, nor did I know how to express my wants to any one for want of English. I only saw one alternative, and that was either to walk all night, or lay down in some field. I preferred the latter, as I was very ill tired, not being much used to walk. Now for the first time, I began to feel deeply that I stood in need of God's mercy. I saw plainly that without it I must perish of hunger in a foreign land. I began to read my evening prayers, and having implored the protection of heaven, I went into a field, made the grass my bed, and was obliged to content myself with the sky for a covering. Sleep, of course, was far from me, nor could I think of any thing but " What shall I do to-morrow ?" While these thoughts were filling my mind, tears filled my eyes, and had I been in a bed I could have said with David—" I watered my couch with my tears," for they were truly flowing in streams from my eyes, and for some time I gave myself up to despair, and, like the Israelites of old, for all God had brought me safe so far, I could not trust in him, but wished I had sunk in the ocean, rather than I should die of hunger here, as it were in a wilderness ; but considering again that it was of no use wishing what might have been, I turned from despondency to prayer, and entreated God to have mercy on me, vowing at the same time, to live in his fear, and keep his commandments all the days of my life, if he would help me out of my great distress. The Lord's hand was not short, nor was his ear heavy that he could not hear ;" for "he heard the voice of my calling, and supplied my wants: I was brought low, and he helped me." As soon as daylight appeared, I arose from my hard bed, and proceeded on my journey. About six o'clock, I laid my phylacteries, and began to say the morning prayers.*

* Phylacteries are two in number ; one for the head, which is called by the Jews, " *Tephillin shell rosh ;*" the other for the hand, and is called, " *Tephillin shell yad.*" These phylacteries are made by Jewish Professors of writing in Hebrew, who are called "scribes." They make the phylacteries of parchment in the shape of four-squared boxes. The boxes differ in size, as they are made from one inch, to three or four inches square. In these boxes are enclosed slips of parchment. The phylactery for the head contains four slips, with select passages of Scripture written on them ; the whole of which passages end with the words—"Thou shalt bind them for a sign upon thy hand, and they shall be as frontlets between thine eyes," from which words the rabbies have invented the phylacteries. The whole of the Scriptures these parchments contain may be found as follows : Deut. vi. 4—9; Exodus xiii. 1—9, and 10—16; Deut. xi. 13—18. The phylactery for the hand contains the same passages of Scripture, only they are all written on *one* slip of parchment. The phylacteries are used only by the males, who do not commence using them until they are thirteen years of age, as the rabbies think before that age children are not capable of handling them with reverence ; and besides, should they by chance drop them on the floor,

My circumstances affected me deeply, and caused me to weep most bitterly for my unfaithfulness to God.* Having got to the prayers called "*Shmowneh esry*," eighteen graces, as the custom is with the Jews, I stood with my face to the east, repeating them, when a gentleman in a gig came driving up. I did not turn round to look at him, as it is considered very sinful to do so at prayers among the Jews. The gentleman it appears stopped when he observed me, for when I had done my prayers, I found him standing close to my back. He asked me several questions, which I could scarcely understand, but I fancied he asked, " what are you weeping for?" Me no Englishman, I said.

they could not fast twenty-four hours, as the rabbinical law requires in that case. To each of the phylacteries a soft leather tape is fastened, about three or four yards in length. To the head phylactery the tape is so fastened, that when the phylactery is fixed on the forehead between the eyes, the two ends of the tape are brought behind the head, and tied in a knot, (when this knot is once tied so as to fit the head, it is not necessary to untie it again, but may carefully be slipped on to the head when going to use them,) and so they are worn, observing to bring the remainder of the tape over the shoulders from behind the head, to hang down in front of the body. And to the hand phylactery, one end of the tape is fastened in a running knot, so that when it is put on to the arm, it may be slackened or pulled tight at convenience. This phylactery is worn on the bare left arm, a little above the elbow, where it is fastened; the remainder of the tape, after putting it round the arm seven times, is brought down to the palm of the hand, round which it is wrapped in the shape of three Hebrew letters that signify the Almighty, viz. Schin, Daleth, Jod. The phylacteries are worn only at morning prayers, whether in public or private, and only on *week* days. In the prayers, when the wearers of the phylacteries meet with a word which they think refers to phylacteries, they touch them with the right hand fingers, and then kiss their fingers. They also observe to kiss the phylacteries at going to use them, and putting them away.

* See page the 12th.

" What are these ?" pointing to the phylacteries. *Tephillin*, I replied. " Are you a Jew ?" Me Jew, yes, Sir. " You believe in Jesus Christ ?" Me Jew, Sir. Seeing he could not make out any thing in conversation, he bought several things of me, and departed. I looked at my money over and over again, and could scarcely believe my eyes that I had taken three shillings so early in the morning. But I blessed the providence of God, feeling truly thankful that he had heard my cries. I was quite astonished when the gentleman asked me whether I believed in Jesus Christ; for in our country one may travel for weeks, and never be asked such a question; but being afraid that it was a sin to talk or think of it, I would not for some time allow even the thought of Christ to enter my mind. I found, however, as I travelled along, that such questions were put to me many times in a day, and made me often wish I understood the Christian doctrine, that I might be better able to reason against it. At length, I became so desirous to know Christianity, that in all the places where I lodged, I inquired after it. But, oh! how greatly was I disappointed in this way of seeking a knowledge of the Christian religion, for all the persons with whom I lodged seemed to me to be as ignorant of it as I was myself. So dangerous is sin, that even in this country where the light of Divine truth blazes in every town and village, it hardens the heart, and blinds the understanding of those who love not the gospel.

Nothing particular occurred after this in my journey

to Birmingham, where I arrived about three weeks after I had left London.

I now took a survey of my stock, and found to the rejoicing of my heart, that I had earned about fifteen shillings above my expences. I felt thankful to the God of Jacob, and could scarcely doubt when the Jews here said to me, "You'll drive your own carriage yet."

With the direction of my Jewish friends, I renewed my stock in the town, and continued in and round about Birmingham for some months, during which time I lived in some degree according to the resolutions I had formed, and this did not only induce the Jews to be my friends, but I also procured the blessing of the God of my fathers upon my stores. My stock was rapidly increasing, even to the envy of those who had been in England much longer than myself; in short, I was doing uncommonly well.

But, oh! how dangerous is prosperity, if we bear not in mind the Source whence all our blessings flow. I had got so far on, that my bread was given me, and my water was sure. I had raiment to put on, and a place where to lay my head, a good stock, and a little money. But I did not keep in view the pit whence I was dug, nor Him that lifted me up. My heart began to be vain, and ready to say, "My power, and the might of my hand hath gotten me all this wealth." I did not feel myself any longer beholden to the mercy of God. I began to neglect my devotion, forgot the vows I had made, and having thus forgotten my God, I found that he was also forgetting me.

I now went to Bristol, and I did so very badly in business that in a short time, I became as poor as ever. Here I was taken ill, and being unable to bear my expences, I was hurried to the hospital, where I laid time enough to bethink myself of my folly, and own the righteous judgment of God.

My own people the Jews, shewed extraordinary kindness to me, during my illness. Several times they collected money for me, and as I durst not eat any of the provision which the hospital provided, (being prohibited by the Talmudical law,) they sent me three very good meals every day I remained there. May God reward their kindness, by enlightening their minds, and removing all that prejudice from their hearts, which hinders them from knowing the truth of redeeming grace! I cannot help here admiring the wisdom of God, in thus attaching the Jews to one another, and making them feel for one another's misfortunes. Indeed, I cannot see what would become of the poorer part of them, if this were not the case. Christians in general think that the Jews are a very rich people, and therefore excuse themselves either from assisting, or encouraging them in business; and many of them are not ashamed to think it their duty, to treat a Jew with contempt because they are under the curse of God.— But ought not this rather to excite sympathy for them ? Ought it not to prompt endeavours to restore them to the favour of God, and to bring them into the fold under Christ the Shepherd ? It is true that God, for their unrepented transgressions, has scattered them all over the earth; yet this affords no reason to Christians to add to their affliction. It cannot, and never will justify them. It was an expression of Frederick, King of Prussia, a most determined enemy of all religion; "I have learned by the experience of ages, that no man ever injured that people but he smarted for it;" a remark which the voice of Inspiration, as well as the experience of mankind, has abundantly confirmed. God has declared by his prophets, that, when he revisits his people, and takes away the veil from their hearts, he will judge and punish their oppressors.—"Behold at that time, I will undo all that afflict thee, I will contend with him that contendeth with thee."

After I recovered from my illness, I found myself in most distressing circumstances. It was winter, the weather was cold, and my clothes were nearly worn out; my stock and money were all spent, and to the Jews to whom I was troublesome, in my lengthened illness, I was ashamed to go again.

> "The winter was cold, and I had no rest,
> "And my heart it was cold as it beat in my breast;
> "No father, no mother, no kindred had I,
> "For I was a parentless, wandering boy."

I gladly would have prayed to God, but I had no confidence that he would hear me; for I saw plainly that I had provoked him to anger. One day I happened to observe to the person with whom I lodged, (who was no professor of religion,) that it was for neglecting to use my phylacteries that I was suffering want, when he replied, "do as I do when I go to the church." And how is that? said I. He replied, say you are sorry for what you did yesterday, and that you'll do better to-day. As I saw no alternative, I took courage, and again determined to cease to do evil, and learn to do well.

In this house there was a person whom I may call a "genteel beggar," he wrote petitions to various gentlemen in the town stating his necessities, and consequently, became acquainted with the dispositions of those to whom he wrote. He remarked to me one day, there is a gentleman who is one of the Society of Friends, and who is so kind hearted, that I believe if he knew your case, he would be glad to have an opportunity to assist you. If you will, I'll write a few lines for you to him, by way of a petition. I felt thankful for the offer, and accepted it. He very soon completed his undertaking, and I proceeded with it to this Gentile friend.

But when I came to the door, I could not for shame to enter, as it was so different a mode of begging from that which is practised among the Jews. To them I needed no ceremony, but plainly and plumply to go in, and say I'm a distressed Israelite, and they understood what was wanted. Three different times I attempted to deliver the petition before I could decide.—"What can I do for thee?" said the Friend. What you please, Sir, said I. "I'll give thee a little matter," and he presented me with half-a-crown. I'm very thankful said I, but I'd rather you would *lend* me a crown than give me half-a-crown, as it would be of more service to me. With five shillings, continued I, I might begin of trading, but not so well with two and sixpence. Having made some observations to me on the Christian faith, he lent me five shillings, and hoped God would enlighten my mind. His countenance expressed a doubting smile, when 1 said 1 would repay him.

1 laid out my five shillings to the best advantage, and the very next day left Bristol, for Bridgewater. Though 1 tried at many houses, 1 could not sell any thing during that day. 1 had eaten very little the whole day, and both my spirits and my strength failed me, and 1 sat down on a heap of stones on the road side to rest, and to weep over my fate, which to me seemed very hard.

While I was thus weeping, and breathing wishes to God for my welfare, a man came up to me who was rather meanly clad, and whose appearance was far from being inviting. He said, "what do you cry for ?" I have six miles to go before 1 can meet with any assistance, and I am very ill tired. " Why, have you friends at Bridgewater ?" No, Sir, but there are Jews in that town, and they will help me, when I get there. " Why do not you go to yonder large house ? It is probable you would get some help there." I never go to ask any thing of Christians, because they say " Bloody Jew." "1 am sure the gentleman who lives there will not say so to you, you had better go." No, Sir, I won't. " Will you, if I go with you ?" So saying, he took me by the hand, and led me on. But oh ! how was I astonished to see him open the front door of the magnificent house, with a key from his pocket. As 1 at once perceived he was the master of it, I began to apologize to him, for my behaviour, but he had no desire to hear me. A footman soon appeared with a lunch tray, well stored with provision, of which my conductor desired me to partake. I was obliged, however, again to say, there is nothing on this tray that I may eat but the bread.* He was very sorry; but learning that I would eat cheese, he ordered it to be brought. He now left me to myself, and said he would return in a few minutes. I was so astonished that I could scarcely eat any thing; however I felt thankful. He appeared again in about ten minutes, and expressed his wonder that I had eaten so very little, and begged I would take some of the bread and cheese with me. He put some of it into a paper, and put it into my hands, together with half-a-crown. I expressed my thanks, took my leave and departed. But to the God of the fatherless, I poured out my utmost gratitude, that he had so providentially helped me in the time of need.

I only stayed one night at Bridgewater, and another

* Many Christians suppose that a Jew will eat any thing set before him, so long as it is not swine's flesh, but this is a gross mistake; for the Jews must not eat any flesh meat whatsoever unless the animal has been killed by a Jew butcher, and in the Jewish way. The rabbi generally acts as a butcher. After he has said the proper grace, he has nothing more to do at the beast than cut its throat, and cut away all the main veins, which he very readily knows where to find, being brought up to it. Then he leaves it to the care of the Christian butcher, with his stamp on it, unless there be a Jew that keeps a butcher's shop. They bring the beast to the ground without knocking it down, as Christians do, and cut its throat at once, that all the blood may be spilt on the ground, as the law requires; and that the beast may have as little pain as possible, the priest sets his knife which he has for that purpose, the same as a razor, and kills the beast generally in one cut. If a Jew says he eats any kind of flesh, if it be not swine's flesh, it may be taken for granted that he is not a religious Jew, and would even eat swine's flesh, if he thought the Christians did not know of it being forbidden.

at Taunton, when I proceeded to Exeter. Here I received seven shillings from the "Jewish Poor Strangers' Fund," and a number of donations from the Jews that reside in the town: so that I was again enabled to lay in a nice little stock of hardware, and again do business with my spirits renewed; and as I was travelling in Devonshire and Cornwall, the Jews so kindly assisted me, that I was very soon raised higher than I was before my illness at Bristol.

In this part of the country I travelled about a long time, until I again felt disposed to visit Bristol and Birmingham. I was doing very well in business, and with a degree of pleasure I reflected, as I travelled towards Bristol, on the change that had taken place in my circumstances, since my friend, the Quaker, lent me five shillings; but I gave God the glory, "who found me, as it were, in a desert land, and led me about, and instructed me, who kept me as the apple of his eye." The day after I arrived in Bristol, I remembered my friend, and went to see him. You do not know me, Sir, I think. "Nay, I know thee not: who art thou, friend?" Do not you remember a poor Jew boy, to whom you lent five shillings? "What is it thou? I'm glad to see thee: how art thou?" I am very well, Sir, and am happy that I am able to return you the five shillings with interest. So saying, I put half a sovereign into his hand. "Nay, friend," said he, "take the whole back, I do not want the principal, and it is my interest to see thee doing well." I am very much obliged to you, Sir, that you consider it your interest to see me doing well, but I beg you will take back your five shillings; I remember you rather doubted of seeing it again. "And how dost thou get thy living now?" I reckon to deal in jewellery, and with your leave will call to-morrow, and shew you how rich I became with your five shillings. "Do so, friend, I shall be glad to see thee. Fare thee well."

I called the next day on this kind friend, who admired my stock, and laid out a considerable sum of money with me. In Bristol I staid some time, and so well was I doing, that I forgot all my past troubles and tears. Such was the influence of my prosperity upon my evil heart.

Oh! how well was Moses acquainted with the depravity of mankind. He says, "When Jeshurun waxed fat, he kicked, he forsook God who made him, and lightly esteemed the Rock of his salvation." This was my own case: when I was surrounded by difficulties, I saw myself little and vile, and thought highly of God; but when fortune came to smile on me, and I saw my way as it were plain before me, I was ready to say, "Soul, take thine ease, eat, drink, and be merry, for thou hast goods laid up for many years." I forgot that the hand which gave, could also take away. As I was travelling from Bristol to Birmingham, I grew so careless about devotion, that I seldom used my phylacteries, and sometimes I never thought that I had such things in my possession, though I had not much prospect of doing well independently of religion.*

* Some of my Christian readers will perhaps wonder that I, who

1 arrived in Birmingham in prosperity, having a much finer stock than when 1 left it. 1 looked upon myself as a very clever young man, and when 1 saw those who were not doing so well as myself, 1 thought it was because they were not as wise, nor as active as 1 was; and when any one admired my good fortune, 1 was not ashamed to say, "All might do as well if they had their wits about them," and little thought that 1 should soon be pennyless. 1 remained in Birmingham for some time, going occasionally to the Warwickshire, and sometimes to the Staffordshire fairs, when 1 was aware of their taking place. One Sunday morning, as 1 stood in Dudley-street, 1 overheard two persons speaking, when one of them said, " Newcastle fair begins to-morrow." 1 took advantage of it, and determined to get ready, and go to the fair. 1 invited two countrymen of mine to go along with me,* and we set off about two o'clock that day with an intention to walk the whole of Sunday night, as it was forty-two miles distant, and we wished to be there at the commencement of the fair. We arrived there the next morning in good time, and 1 proceeded to the place where 1 used to lodge when 1 was there before, but found it occupied; and as 1 had a wish to make the

am now a professor of Christianity, should dwell so much on the use of the phylacteries, and enlarge so much on the neglect of them; but they will remember the words of the Apostle, "that those who live under the law will be judged by it." If the Jews, therefore, think the use of the phylacteries incumbent upon them as a law, the neglect of them subjects them to the condemnation of the law.

* One of them has since embraced Christianity at Glasgow.

best of the fair, I went out for business immediately, though 1 was very ill tired. 1 did very well at the fair all the day. In the afternoon, 1 met a Jew boy in the market-place, who accosted me with a Jewish "how do you do?" (*Sholom alychem?*) 1 gave him my hand, and returned the compliment. 1 asked him, if he could tell me where I could lodge that night? He believed 1 could lodge at the black-horse public house. We proceeded there, and by way of expressing my thanks for his trouble, 1 called for a quart of ale, and set down my box on the floor beside my feet, between myself and my companion; and not having had rest the night before, 1 unconsciously gave way to sleep. How long 1 slept 1 know not, but when 1 awoke, 1 found both my box and my companion were gone. 1 screamed, and tore my hair, but all to no purpose. To complete my misfortune, all the money 1 had taken that day was in copper, and to save my pockets, 1 had locked it up in my box, so that all my money was also gone. It is rather remarkable that a week before this, another traveller was robbed of his box, and when he stated that he had money in it, 1 could not believe it. The scene of this misfortune 1 am scarcely able to describe, for when 1 found myself reduced from a gentleman to a beggar, as it were in the twinkling of an eye, such despair and confusion got hold of me, that many believed 1 should lose my senses. My companions who came with me from Birmingham, were but very poor themselves; however, when they found me in the market, destitute of every thing, they immediately offered me all the assistance in their pow-

D

er, which was a shilling. I ran also to a Jew who lives there, with my complaints, who gave me a little money, and informed me of the name of the author of my calamity, and of the residence of his relations.* He also drew up on a sheet of paper, the sum of my misfortunes, and himself and his family signed it, with which, he particularly wished me to call on a relation of his in Manchester. The whole of this night I spent in tears, bemoaning my wretched fate. This calamity I did not take as usual; I did not consider it as a punishment for my offences; but thought misfortune was always to be *my* lot. "O God", I said, "why died I not from the womb? why did I not give up the ghost when I was born? for now should I have lain still and quiet, where the wicked cease from troubling, and the weary are at rest." Such thoughts as these came in floods on my mind, and for some time I could not reconcile myself to my fate.

Now the season came on when the Jews celebrate their new year, and the great atonement days, and I hastened to Manchester in order to attend the Synagogue at these solemn feasts. The Jew, whose relation lives at Newcastle, and to whom I had an introductory letter, received me with great kindness. He invited me to eat at his house the new year feasts, and assisted me with money; and when I told him the history of my past misfortunes, he hoped I would ardently pray for a better

* My readers will excuse me for not naming them, or their residence, as it would be painful to them, and I believe they are all very respectable, this young rogue their son excepted. They live in the county of Norfolk, let this suffice.

fortune to myself in the ensuing year.* This, indeed, afforded me a degree of consolation, as 1 trusted God would grant me better fortune in the coming year. The Jews here made up a collection for me, and 1 laid the money out in goods, and left Manchester, after the holy days, with an intention to go into Norfolk, in hopes of discovering the thief.

As 1 took a long round, it was some months before 1 arrived at the intended place, where 1 very soon found the relations of the wicked youth. He was then at home, and as 1 entered the house I was recognized by him. Before 1 could speak a word he ran away through the back door, and was soon out of sight. 1 was well received by his relations, who greatly regretted my misfortune, and promised to assist me with three or four pounds, if I would proceed against him, as they observed, " he ruins both our character and fortune;" this being neither the first nor second time that he had been found guilty of stealing. He got out of my way three or four different times; but at length I succeeded in taking him into custody in his native town. At the trial he confessed the whole truth, as I have related it, but with so many tears, that myself and the sitting magistrates pitied him, and we forgave him all. He was, however, convicted for another robbery but two days after this, for which he was transported.

1 did not receive the promised sum from his father;

* It is a faith among the Jews, that on the new year and great atonement days, God decrees what shall happen to his people all the year round.

and as my stock was very small, I went about business much out of spirits. 1 travelled about in this town for some time, when 1 proceeded to 1pswich. On my arrival there, 1 called upon a Jewish rabbi, who received me with usual kindness. After some conversation, he said, "1 could put some money into your way, if the manner of getting it would not be disagreeable to you." 1 will do any thing, if it be not stealing. "Well," he said, "a Jewish lady died here this morning, and her last wish was that two Jews should watch within sight of her sepulchre for the first four nights after her burial, and if you like to be one of the two, you will be well rewarded." 1 said 1 had no objection, provided he would lend me a prayer-book to use during the night.*

On the day appointed for her burial, I waited at the burial ground to see her interred, as I never before witnessed an interment. It is impossible for me to express what 1 felt at the sight of her corpse and shroud,† particularly when I considered that

> So will the fairest face appear,
> When youth and years are flown:
> Such is the robe that kings must wear,
> When death has 'reft their crown.

* The Jews consider the burial-ground a most solemn and awful place, and would never pass one at twelve o'clock at night, if they could possibly avoid it, as they believe the dead awake at that time, and go to prayers in the Synagogue. Their fear is, however, diminished, if they are provided with *tsitsith*, and proper prayers. Good *tsitsith* I had, but I wanted a prayer-book.

† Among the Jews the coffins are not made up until they are at the grave side, and are just going to inter the corpse, as they believe that the dead can hear and perceive their caresses, until the third shovel full of earth has been thrown upon the coffin.

1 felt myself as a creature born to die, and that one day might bring me to the dust whence 1 sprung. I said, What is all my anxiety? Why do 1 long for riches? If I had them, what could they do for me in my dying hour? Why do I so deeply regret the loss of my stock? Can I take it with me when 1 die? Ah, no! like this poor woman, I must leave every thing behind me, if 1 have ever so much, and empty and lonely, I must go to the grave.

In a house near the cemetry, the window of which gave full sight of the various sepulchres, we took our station for watching the new grave. We both were in a very serious mood, and when we thought on the end of all living, we resolved to live in a manner becoming good Jews. This, as well as the three following nights, 1 spent in reading various meditations and prayers, and formed one resolution after another that whatever other Jews did, I would serve the God of my fathers. As I was expecting to receive a pound for watching, 1 prayed God to enable me to get a living with it, and he heard my prayers once more; for he is merciful, and doth not keep his anger for ever. The moment he perceives his people desirous to return, he is ready to embrace them; no sooner does he see the prodigal afar off, than he runs to meet him; " and as a father pitieth his children, so the Lord pitieth them that fear him." Many will wonder that 1, who experienced so much of God's justice and mercy, should be so prone to evil; but they will remember, that " the heart of man is deceitful above all things, and desperately wicked." If this had not been the case; would the Saviour have repeated so often as he did, " Watch ?"   It must also be remembered that 1 was without Christ, and "without Him we are nothing."   Having done my duty as a watchman, 1 received a pound for my hire, with which I increased my stock, and endeavoured to try my fortune again.   I travelled through Bedfordshire with great success; and in Northamptonshire I earned more money than ever I did in my life before, in the same time. Fortune again began to smile on me. I succeeded better every day, and I looked upon myself again as being somebody in the world.   Before I arrived at Birmingham, I provided myself with a new suit of clothes, so that when 1 got there, I joined the most fashionable travellers at the " Green Man," and they had no objection to my company while I had money.

Having spent much time in pleasure, all the serious impressions I had received at Ipswich were drowned. I now resumed my travelling again, and proceeded to Manchester, doing all I could with my business in Staffordshire, and 1 did remarkably well.   But this I little deserved, for I now lived in a most shameful neglect of my religion, and seldom or never prayed. While 1 prospered so well in business, 1 lived as though God had forgotten me, and did not see all my sinful works. Oh, how infatuating is sin! how does it blind the heart of man !   It made me the keeper of vineyards, but my own vineyard 1 did not keep.   It led me to forsake the Author of my comfort, the God of my fathers, my Guide, my Preserver, my Helper in time of need, and caused me to put my trust in Baal, in blind chance,

Oh, how feelingly does the prophet express it, "They have forsaken the Lord, they have provoked the Holy One of Israel to anger; they are gone away backward. The ox knoweth his owner, and the ass his master's crib, but Israel doth not know, my people do not consider." Alas! I was too fond of pleasure and gay company to keep in mind the fountain whence I drew water, or to remember the way that God led me in the wilderness. But who could expect that I should long continue with religious desires, even after the last impressions I received? for I attempted all in my own strength, and had nothing more to keep me, than the awful thunders and lightnings that were once seen and heard on Mount Sinai, the terrors of the law, and the misfortunes with which God chastised me at various times.

I now arrived in Manchester in the highest spirits, and was not a little proud when some of the Jews said to me, "what a change! you'll yet be the *Parness* of the Duke's Place Synagogue"* I had now a stock worth about £25., and several pounds in money. This was more than ever I owned in my life before, and I considered myself in a sure way of making a fortune. With a degree of pleasure I used to say, "I must keep my eyes open now, for this is too good a box to have stolen." But God has more ways than one to punish sinners; it is not always necessary to withhold our customers from us, to remind us that we are dependant on Him, nor to allow us to be robbed of our property, to

* Parness is the title given to the second ruler of a Synagogue.

make us humble, nor yet to deprive us of our friends, to convince us that we are dying creatures : his ways are as numerous as the sands on the sea shore ; if one way will not bring a sinner to a sense of his duty, He can try a thousand others. It was thus God dealt with the children of Israel in ancient times, it was thus he dealt with me. "Who hath hardened himself against God, and prospered ? I have not ; but having been called both by mercy and judgment, and having still chosen my own way, and walked contrary unto God, "He also walked contrary unto me in fury." To Manchester I came, dreaming of nothing but pleasure. To past time I would not look ; the present, I did not improve, nor did I meditate on the future, or perhaps I might have expected the troubles, that were just at hand.

Two or three days after I arrived in Manchester, I was taken with illness, which very soon became serious. Being determined to bear my own expences, if possible, I soon found my money was going very quickly, as I was not able to leave my bed, and do business. I also began to sell off my stock to Jewish travellers, and sometimes was obliged to sell articles a great deal under prime cost, in order to have money as fast as I was obliged to spend it. At first it greatly increased my affliction, to see my goods going for next to nothing ; but having learned from one of the doctors one day, that it would become me to think of another world, I had sufficient matter to think about, without thinking of my stock. He said, while examining my pulse, "I am at a loss what to prescribe for you next. You are in the hand of God, he may yet have mercy on you. Did you ever think any thing about Jesus Christ? We believe he is the only Saviour." Doctor, said I, if you think I am dying, torment me not with your Christ. I don't know him, and I will not know him. " I only mean it for your good," the doctor said, " God may perhaps lengthen out your span, but if you believed in Christ"—Leave my room, Sir, I beg: begone, I'll hear no more.

Several Jews came to visit me soon after the departure of the doctor, when I was in tears. Why do you weep, they said, shall we say "*Shema yisroile*," (hear, O Israel,) with you?* O dear friends, will it be of any use, I have not said it this long time. "Did not you say it every day, when you laid your phylacteries?" I have not laid my phylacteries for a long time. They all shook their heads; and I fancied one of them said what a "*Posho yisroile* he has been," (viz. what a wicked Israelite he has been!)

When the Jews departed, I could not help thinking on their last reflection, which though severe, was but too just. I appear the same in the sight of my brethren, I thought, as I do in the sight of God. What will become of me? I am weary of my life, but how can I die, wicked as I am, in the sight of God and man!

* Hear, O Israel, is a prayer used by the Jews twice every day. They believe if a Jew is ever so bad, he will have a portion of paradise, if he has persevered in saying this prayer. They also believe, that invisible foes, or evil spirits, can do them no harm, if they have presence of mind to repeat this prayer, when attacked by them, and they consider themselves happy if they die with *Shemah Yisroile*, on their lips.

The horrors I felt at this time, it is not possible to describe, and I could not help wishing that God would try me once more. I read a great deal in the psalms of David, and I breathed many ejaculations to the long-suffering God, to restore me to health, if it were but for a short time, that I might recover my strength, before I should go hence and be no more seen. The day after this, I was much worse. The sorrows of death compassed me about. I found sorrow and trouble; but blessed be God the pains of hell did not enkindle upon me. In this my unenlightened state, I did not cease to repeat psalms, when I was able, and some of the travellers who visited me prayed with me, *Shemah yisroile,* &c. viz. Hear, O Israel. The next day I felt a little better, and the doctor conceived some hope. O how unwilling is God that any should perish! he would rather that they would turn from their sins, and live; and though for sin, he doth chastise men, yet it is with a fatherly hand, and no sooner does he see them corrected, than he is ready to heal the wounds he has made. I now grew better, and stronger every day; and as soon as I was able I began to lay my phylacteries, for which I was highly commended by the Jews. My illness had now continued six weeks, and my stock was all sold, and even my box. I lingered a few days ere I was able to walk about, and when I had settled with my landlady, I found that I was worth one shilling and sixpence. The Jews here had done already a great deal for me, and I could not expect any thing from them, so I determined on going to Liverpool. I set off early in the morning, and having travelled nearly all day, I arrived in Liverpool much tired. During the day I had spent fifteenpence in refreshment, so I had only three-pence left. I felt as if I could not proceed immediate-ly to the Jews, and I walked up and down in one of the streets, reflecting on my miserable state. What shall I do with this threepence, thought I, shall I pay it for lodgings,* or shall I get something to eat? While musing thus, I wept for sorrow; and while I stood, lost in thought, an old man came by, to whom I said, can you tell me where I can lodge to-night? I do not wish to go to expensive lodgings, for I am very poor. "Expensive or not expensive," replied the old man, "I keep lodgings, and if you like to come along with me you are welcome." This man was a Methodist. I very gladly went with him home, and a chair near the fireside was refreshing to me. He asked me to take a cup of tea with him, of which I never stood more in need. As soon as he perceived me a little refreshed, he drew his chair near to me, and some such conversa-tion as follows took place between us :—

" I think you are not an Englishman." No, Sir, I am not: I am a native of Poland, and was born in Warsaw. "What is the established religion in Poland. are not they all Catholics?" The Catholic religion is the established religion, but the Poles are not all Ca-tholics. There is a great number of Jews in Poland. "And may I ask you to which of these professions you belong?" Well, Sir, I have the honour to belong to

* In threepenny lodgings they always expect payment beforehand.

the Jews. "Of course, it is to your honour in some respects." 'In some respects, Sir! in every respect. Were not the Jews the first people whom God chose? Did he not with wonders bring them out of Egypt? And does not God say to the Jews, "1 am your God, and you are my people? 1t is to my honour to be a Jew, and I am proud to be called one. "O, 1 do not dispute all this, 1 verily believe the Jews were the favourites of God, and they yet will be. But 1 am far from thinking that they are his favourites now, as God has scattered them for their rejection of his plan of salvation." 1 know very well that we are in captivity, but we look for the Messiah, our deliverer, and daily expect his coming. "Here is your mistake; you look for a Messiah which has already appeared." Messiah already appeared! 1f he had, you would not have found me here to night, in want of a few pence. 1 should have been in Jerusalem under my vine and fig-tree. "And so you would, if you had believed in him, but you crucified him. When Pilate was determined to let him go, you said you would not have that man to reign over you. Do you think that Moses could have brought the 1sraelites out of Egypt, if they had determined to remain there? You bring to my mind, the words you quoted when we were coming home, 'Because 1 have called and ye refused, 1 have stretched out my hand and no man regarded, 1 will laugh at your calamities.' He came to deliver you, but you would not be delivered by him." Well, well, 1 have done with you now. The Messiah, the Son of God, to be

crucified! Why did he not save himself from the wicked men and their blood-thirsty hands? The Jews asked him to come down from the cross that they might
believe in him. Why did he not come down? It was
because he could not. "Now, do not be too hasty, if
you'll only have patience, I am confident I can put you
right." Put me right! The more I talk to you, the
more I see myself right: neither you, nor any of the
Christians are right, you are a complete set of idola-
ators, believing a man, that was crucified, to be God, I
would be ashamed to own such a thing! I told you
when we were coming home that I had been near
the gates of death, and that I did not like to die just
then, because I had not used my phylacteries for so
long a time previous to my illness, but I could have
died with more confidence in that state, than die believing in your Christ. I hope to be a good Jew now,
and to lay my phylacteries, and God will forgive me my
past neglect. Let us have no more about your Jesus
Christ. The old man heaved a heavy sigh, and said,
" Dear boy, I am delighted to see you have such a
spirit for defending what you think is just, but I beg
you will listen to me for another minute, while I shall
ask you one or two questions, and, if after I have done,
you should still be resolute in your faith, I will trouble
you no more." I would gladly have refused to hear
him, but I thought it would look very unbecoming of
me, as he was so kind as to take me in, when he knew
I had no money. So I said, well, go on, and he commenced thus. " Will you tell me candidly on what

E

you founded your hopes of being saved from hell, when you felt you deserved it, and thought you were on a dying bed at the same time?" Why, 1 had my hopes in God's mercy. "But if you know that God is merciful, you also know that he is just, and that his justice requires the shedding of blood for the remission of sins." But we cannot sacrifice now, because we are far from the temple. "Here then comes my last question: it is now eighteen hundred years since the Jews sacrificed for sin, and if we believe the law of Moses, that without the shedding of blood there is no remission of sin, then no Jew that has died during the last eighteen hundred years, is saved from the wrath of God. Where now is God's mercy you boast of? or is it consistent with his mercy, to leave the world for so long a period, without providing a plan for saving his people, for saving one Jew?" I was quite astonished, when he had done speaking, and said, 1 must confess it appears quite inconsistent with God's mercy to leave the world altogether without hope. But in ancient time, God declared himself to be merciful. "He is as merciful now as ever he was," replied the old man, "and so you would think, if you would but behold the Lamb of God that taketh away the sin of the world." And what Lamb is that, Sir? "It is Jesus Christ, that was brought as a Lamb to the slaughter. He hath borne our griefs, and carried our sorrows. The Jews esteemed him stricken of God, but he was wounded for our transgressions, he was bruised for our iniquities. Do not look at me, as though 1 was telling you a fable.

See, it is here in the Bible, in the fifty-third chapter of Isaiah." I was quite astonished at his arguments, and I told him that I would think about it, and I would have some more conversation with him some other night. The next day, I went among the Jews, from whom I collected thirty shillings, which I laid out in goods, but did not go out for business, as I felt a wish to speak with my landlord, on the important subject we were on the night before. Now Mr. Ross, I said, I have a hard question for you, and I doubt whether you will answer it. "And what is that?" Why, supposing I grant that the office of the Messiah is to take away the sin of the world, how can you prove that this Messiah is already come? and if he has come, how can you prove that Jesus of Nazareth is the Messiah? "If the question be hard," replied Mr. R., "the answer, however, is easy. That the Messiah is already come, is plain, not merely from the New Testament, but from the Old, See the forty-ninth chapter of Genesis, and tenth verse. "The sceptre shall not depart from Judah, nor a lawgiver from between his feet, until Shiloh come." Now, you must own that the sceptre has departed from Judah. If it had not, the Jews would not be thus scattered all over the world. That the sceptre is departed from Judah is also plain, from the Jews not knowing which of them is of Judah, and which not. If, then, the sceptre has departed from Judah, Shiloh must have come; for the Scriptures expressly say, that it would not depart from Judah until Shiloh should come." I was struck with astonishment at this plain proof, for I had seen this passage of Scripture a hundred times before, but never in so clear a light. I did not, however, interrupt the old man, as I was anxious to hear him prove that Christ was Shiloh. " Now that Jesus was the Messiah," continued Mr. R., "is sufficiently plain, if there were no other evidence, than the sufferings which he underwent, for he suffered according to the Scriptures." I could not refrain any longer, but seized his hand, and said, You'll make me a Christian yet. For the first fortnight in this town, I went but little about business, but searched the Scriptures daily to find whether these things were so.

On my second Sunday in this town, Mr. R. asked me to go with him to a Methodist Chapel, but like Nicodemus, I was afraid of going in the day time, for fear of the Jews : I promised, however, to go with him at night. I had never been at a Christian place of worship before ; and I fancied from what I had heard of the Catholics in Poland, I should find the place crowded with images, and I proceeded towards it with a degree of dislike ; for I thought, whether the Messiah has come or not, they ought not to bow before the works of their own hands. But how greatly was I surprised, when I found, on the opening of the door, that the Methodist Chapel looked plainer than a Jewish Synagogue ! My hair stood upon an end on my head. I trembled for fear ; and with Jacob I felt " the Lord is in this place, and I knew it not ! How dreadful is this place ! This is none other than the house of God." When I entered, the preacher was praying and the people were kneeling. Very becoming posture I thought,* and I knelt down likewise. As I had never before heard a Christian sermon, I could understand but little, however I recognised the expression, " he died for the sin of the world," which the preacher had very often occasion to use, and which I had heard from my landlord. I could scarcely any longer doubt of the truth of Christianity. Indeed, I could not help wishing it was a true faith; for I thought " what a rich provision for a sinful world !" After we returned from the house of God, I said to Mr. R., " I wish I had a situation in some Christian family, that I might learn not only their religion, but also their habits." " This is my own wish for you," said he, " and if you like, I will write to a friend in this town, in your behalf." To this, of course, I consented. He then wrote a letter stating his views of my case, and suggested whether I was not a proper object for the notice of "the Society for the promotion of Christianity among the Jews." When the letter was finished, Mrs. R. took it to Mr. Pearson, and he shewed it to the Rev. W. Clegg, who agreed with him, that I should be requested to come to Mr. P.'s house, on Wednesday night, when Mr. C. with some other friends, would attend, and inquire into my case, and adopt such measures as they might think best for my spiritual and temporal welfare. On Tuesday night, Mr. R. took me with him to a Class Meeting, and when we got there, he introduced me to the meeting as an inquiring Jew. I was rather

* The Jews stand or sit at prayer.

E 3

surprised, when every one present shook hands with me. 1 thought, at first, that they did it out of custom, but 1 found they all remembered me in their prayers. 1 approved of the meeting, and said to the leader, "1 hope not to be a stranger here."

The following night, 1 went with Mr. R. to Mr. Pearson's, where 1 found Mr. Clegg, with several other gentlemen, waiting for my appearance. After they had all shook hands with me, 1 sat down among them, and a great number of inquiries were made, with the view of ascertaining the sincerity of my profession. When they were satisfied, Mr. P. consented to take me into his house, until it could be ascertained whether the society before mentioned, would take me under their care, and, with the understanding that 1 should have liberty to call on Mr. C. two or three times a week, to increase my Christian knowledge.* About eight o'clock, the servant brought the supper in, when 1 began to look at myself from head to foot, and 1 thought surely they are not going to have this poor boy to supper with them. 1 was, however, soon convinced to the contrary, when they asked me to come to the table. This was the first time of my taking a Christian meal, and 1 could not help admiring this act of real kindness, considering 1 was altogether an alien to them.

* Mr. Clegg now mentioned my case to the Rev. T. Tattershall, minister of St. Augustine's, and Secretary to the above Society, in Liverpool, who, after he had written in my behalf to the Society, was informed in answer, that they refused to take persons of my age, as they had met with many impositions.

Having agreed to enter into Mr. P.'s employment, and to come the following morning, Mr. R. and myself departed. The next day, 1 went to Mr. P.'s and was glad that 1 had the opportunity, as 1 hoped, of learning to earn my bread with less temptation, and to adorn my religious profession.

Soon after this, the Secretary of the Liverpool Bible Society introduced me to the Rev. T. Tattershall, who kindly lent me a Hebrew Bible, which 1 found very useful, as the temptation was sometimes presented to my mind, that perhaps the Christians had invented their Bible to answer their own ends. By the kindness of Mr. Clegg, 1 had been previously furnished with a Hebrew Testament, so that having now the whole Scriptures in my own language, 1 could seek out any things which appeared difficult to me, and lay them before my two friends who were always ready to give me instruction and encouragement. 1 am astonished at the trouble 1 took the liberty to give them, as 1 used to call on each of them very frequently, for several months together. By their private instructions, by regularly attending the preaching of the gospel, by constantly meeting in the Class of Mr. John Hughes, and by my own careful reading, study and prayer, my judgment became perfectly convinced that 1 had found Him of whom Moses in the law, and the prophets did write. 1 then fancied 1 was in a fit state for making a public profession of my faith, by attending to the holy ordinance of Baptism. 1 therefore propose it several times to Mr. Clegg; but, contrary to my expectations, he always contrived to " put it off a little longer." 1 then mentioned it to Mr. Tattershall, but meeting with no better success from him, 1 became prejudiced against them, and determined not to solicit them again ; thinking if they should wish aftewards to baptize me, they should ask me.   In this prejudice 1 remained for some time, and might have continued till now, if the Lord, in mercy, had not taken away the veil from my heart, and given me to see, not only the pure motives of these worthy ministers, but my utter unworthiness of becoming a member of the Christian church.

One Sunday night, 1 was at Pitt-Street Chapel, when Mr. Clegg was to preach ; and when he was about to give out the text, 1 looked at him steadfastly that 1 might not miss hearing it, when 1 fancied that his eyes were fixed upon me.   But what was my astonishment at hearing him pronounce for his text, " Judas, betrayest thou the Son of Man with a kiss ?" He may well refuse to baptize me, said 1, if he thinks I am like Judas : now he has just chosen this for his text because 1 am here. But although 1 felt greatly mortified, I was determined to hear all he had to say against me, only I had made up my mind that it should not disturb me in the least. But, wonderful to relate, that though I had shut up my heart against conviction, yet the Lord had mercy on me.   He did not give me up to my own evil will : he did not say, " Let him alone, for he is joined to his idols;" but he spoke to me with that voice which wakes the dead, and bids the sleeper rise."   He shewed me what I was by nature, and what I must be by grace. He accompanied the word preached with his Spirit, and it came with power to my heart. Before the sermon was half done, I saw myself in the very character of Judas; I was owning the Saviour with a kiss, yet denying him by my works. I stood condemned in the sight of God and man, for I still believed Mr. C. was addressing me, and seeing myself sinful to the utmost, and unworthy to be numbered in the Church of God, I was obliged to own at the footstool of mercy, that I bore these two good men, hatred without a cause.

When the sermon was over, I went home to my chamber and looked at various forms of prayer I had in my possession; but not finding any to answer the feelings of my heart, I fell down on my knees before God, and offered the Publican's prayer. I confessed before God, that I had crucified the Saviour afresh, and put him to open shame. In this state of mind I was nearly three weeks, doubting the sufficiency of God's mercy. I believed Christ died for the sin of the world, yet could not rely on him as having died for me.

On Good Friday morning, as I was going to the chapel, I reflected on the events that took place on Calvary. I saw the bleeding Saviour, I looked on him whom I had pierced by my sins, and mourned, and my soul melted into tears. I was now ready to hear the preacher explain the sufferings of Christ according to the Scripture. He took for his text, "Thus it is written, and thus it behoved Christ to suffer, and to rise from the dead the third day, and that repentance and remission of sins should be preached in his name, among all nations, beginning at Jerusalem." The first part of this subject was pleasing to me, as 1 was fully convinced that Christ had suffered according to prediction. But the last part was to me joy unspeakable, and full of glory. When he was explaining the words, "beginning at Jerusalem," and was remarking that Christ sent his first offer of pardon to the people of Jerusalem, to those who drove the nails into his hands and feet, to that very man who pierced his side, I could no longer doubt the sufficiency of the atonement for my soul. "Surely," said 1, "if 1 have pierced him with my crimes, he still offers pardon to me.

> God is love, I know, I feel,
> Jesus weeps and loves me still."

Having now left my burden at the cross of Christ, 1 went home, rejoicing in the God of my salvation. 1 felt happier now when 1 rejoiced in the Saviour's love, than ever 1 had felt in my life, and 1 poured out my ardent thanksgivings to my pardoning God, determining, at the same time, to be guided by his counsel, and influenced by his Spirit, in all my actions. Having gone on in this delightful path of religion, for some time, finding grace and strength according to my day, Mr. C. thought, at length, 1 might be baptized; and 1 rejoiced at the prospect of confessing the Saviour before many witnesses. Sunday, the first of October, 1826, was appointed to be the day when this solemn ceremony should be performed, in Pitt-Street Chapel. In the forenoon, at half-past ten o'clock, the service was opened as usual, by singing a hymn, and prayer, and after the lessons were read, Mr. C. introduced me to the congregation, and asked me to give them an account of the manner in which 1 was led to embrace the Christian faith. With the assistance of God's grace, 1 was enabled to relate the history of my conversion, to the edification of the hearers. After this, Mr. C. asked me several very important questions, from the Baptism of Adults, in the Book of Common Prayer, with some others peculiar to my case, all of which 1 answered according to the grace given me. Mr. C. now gave me a most solemn address, exhorting me to perseverance, &c. When this was finished, he baptized me in the name of the Father, Son, and Holy Ghost, and offered up an appropriate and earnest prayer in my behalf. 1 felt now more cause for rejoicing than ever, seeing myself joined to the Christian Church, and acknowledged by them as a member of that fold, over which Christ alone is the shepherd. A sermon was now preached by Mr. C. most admirably adapted for the important occasion, from the following text: "But this 1 confess unto thee, that after the way which they call heresy, so worship 1 the God of my fathers, believing all things which are written in the law and in the prophets." Acts xxiv. 14. I felt highly gratified, and 1 believe so were all the congregation, at the evidence Mr. C. brought forward in my behalf; showing that by believing in Christ, 1 worshipped the God of my fathers, and believed all things which are written in the law and in the prophets. When the service was over, I went home, and while 1 there poured out my gratitude to God, for the wonders he had wrought in me, I pleaded with him in behalf of his people, the Jews, who are in darkness and in the shadow of death, perishing for lack of knowledge. And 1 particularly prayed for my dear parents and relations, who have often daringly blasphemed the Saviour of the world. O that God would remember them in mercy!

> Lord, send thy word to that far land,
>   Where my poor brethren dwell;
> Teach them the way, the truth, the life,
>   That saves from sin and hell.
>
> Oh! that my father, mother dear,
>   Might there thy mercy see!
> Might know what Christ has done for them,
>   What Christ has done for me!

I also prayed while at the throne of grace, that God would make my way plain before me, and that he would direct all my paths; for 1 was well aware of many of the difficulties I should have to encounter when I determined to follow Christ. 1 knew that my father and mother would cast me off, and that 1 should become a stranger, yea an alien to my mother's children, and 1 stood in need not only of direction in my path, but of strength to walk in it.

Having briefly related my history until my baptism, 1 thought of concluding; but as some of my readers may be desirous of knowing something of my life since my conversion, 1 will rapidly run over the principal circumstances.

When 1 learned that the London Society declined taking me under their care, for reasons already stated, Mr. Clegg, and a few others who wished me well, complied with my inclinations, and bound me an apprentice to a watch movement maker. I liked the business very much, but circumstances were such, that my friends thought it best that a separation should take place, and my master and myself having mutually agreed upon it, the indenture was destroyed in the presence of Mr. C.

With the assistance of my leader, Mr. Hughes, I was afterwards bound an apprentice to a hair-dresser, who was a member of the Methodist society. In this place, I was very comfortable; and, with a degree of pleasure, I used to reflect on the innocence of my employment, thinking if ever I should be able to maintain myself by this business, it would be getting a living honestly in the sight of men. 1 lived in this place about ten months, when my master gave up the business, began the cotton trade, and left the town. Thus I was again left to shift for myself. There were only two others of the business who kept the Sabbath day holy, and they either would not, or could not take me. As 1 would not bind myself to Sabbath-breakers, 1 was obliged to think of some other business. About this time, Mr. Butterfield, a young gentleman from Keighley, was on a visit at Mr. Clegg's, who wanted a footman. Mr. C. recommended me to him; and he agreed to take me. He immediately called in a tailor, procured for me a suit of clothes, and was the first who offered me wages. He took me with him to Manchester during the Conference, and having stopped a month there, he took me to my new home at Keighley. 1 lived with him a year, during which time, except a few trials I met with from persons who took pleasure in reproaching me for being a descend- ant of Jews, 1 was very comfortable; but my master determining not to keep a footman any longer, 1 was dismissed. 1 was mortified at being so unfortunate, but 1 hoped that the God of the fatherless would not suffer me to be tried more than 1 was able to bear, but would make a way for my escape. A fellow-servant advised me to make my circumstances known to the Rev. T. Dury, Rector of Keighley, as he was a very humane man. 1 took her advice, and told Mr. D. that my master was going to travel without a footman, and that 1 should be left without a situation. He said he would call on my master to ascertain my character, and then he would do for me what he could. When I call- ed on him again, he told me he would write to some of his friends in my behalf, and if I did not meet with a situation by the time 1 should leave Mr. B., 1 might come to his house until 1 met with one. 1 was truly thankful to God, that he had disposed the heart of a stranger to be my friend, for 1 had very little know- ledge of Mr. Dury before. 1t is a true saying, that " a friend in need is a friend indeed." When my time was up with Mr. B., Mr. Dury welcomed me to his house, and when 1 had lived with him a month, he procured for me a situation as footman with F. J. Lace,

Esq. of lngthorpe-Grange, near Skipton. Mr. D. paid me full wages for the month I was with him, though he did not want me; and after he had given me some very good advice, respecting my conduct, as a servant and a Christian, I departed.   I could not, however, leave without regret; for I was leaving a kind master and friend, and a good mistress, and very agreeable fellow-servants.   But blessed be God, whose compassions fail not, in my new place, I also found kind Christian people, and was liberally treated both by my master and mistress. For besides the religious privileges 1 enjoyed in the house, (as we had family prayer morning and evening every day, and a sermon read or preached by the master every Sunday night,) I had leave to attend a class meeting, and any other religious meeting, when I could spare time. I lived in this family very comfortably, but not without many trials of my faith, one or two of which 1 may mention :—Once 1 was so unfortunate as to break a bottle of port wine, and, as 1 had broken several other things in the same week, I was ashamed to own the accident, and was tempted to fabricate a falsehood about it.   But, a short time before my varacity was to be put to the test, we went out to dine at the Rev. W. Worsney's, of Fence-End, and, after 1 had done waiting at the table, and sat down in the servants' hall, 1 took hold of a volume of tracts, written by Mrs. H. More. On opening it, I fixed my attention on a tract entitled—"*Charles Jones, the Footman,*" in which 1 met with the following striking anecdote of

Charles Jones :—He was sent one day by his master, who was a clergyman, with a bottle of wine to a sick woman in the parish, and, by some means, he broke the bottle in his way, and did not know what to do; but determined, at length, to hide the misfortune from his master, by telling him that he delivered the wine, and that the woman was thankful for it, and that she was a little better. Going along with these thoughts, he met a pedlar who was selling tracts, and bought one of him, which was on the subject of lying. The reading of it, under the blessing of God, was the means of convincing him of the awfulness of the crime he was about to perform. He went home and told the truth, and, not many minutes afterwards, a person came to the minister and informed him, that the woman had been dead for some time. C. J. was then glad that he had told the truth, and saved himself from disgrace. 1 was astonished that 1 should have met with this anecdote, at so particular a time, and plainly saw it was a warning from God, and 1 resolved to tell the truth. Next day, I took an opportunity to acquaint my master with the accident, and told him how 1 had been tempted to deceive him, and of the tract 1 read at Mr. Worsney's. He did not blame me, but kindly said, be thankful to God, that he enabled you to confess your fault. I was indeed thankful, for now my conscience was at ease, and my prayer was that the Lord, in future, would

Arm me with jealous care,
As in his sight to live.

At another time, I met with a very severe temptation, which almost proved my ruin. Reading one day the eleventh of St. Matthew, 1 began to feel uneasy at the particular message of John the Baptist to Christ. "What," said 1, " the Baptist ignorant whether Jesus was the Messiah or not? He that cried 'behold the Lamb,' not to know whether this was the Messiah, he that heard the voice from heaven witnessing that Jesus was the well-beloved, in whom God was well pleased, to doubt whether this was the Messiah? John, whom Christ pronounced to be Elias, not to know who was the Messiah? Who should know, if he did not? He was afraid, he was deluded; and very likely he was, and are not all Christians under delusion? Have not 1 been deluded most foolishly myself?" Such infidel thoughts crowded my mind, and it was not long before I became secretly an unbeliever, and looked back with abhorrence on the professions 1 had made. 1 neglected my closet, nor did 1 attend to my class, to the extreme sorrow of my leader, who was one of my fellow-servants. I did not reveal to him my reasons for absenting myself from the class, considering him a poor deluded soul, walking in the dark, not knowing where: nor did I ever mention this to my master, who would have taken great pleasure in putting me right, from a notion 1 had, that no one was able to do it. In this way to destruction 1 was for several weeks, but not without fear on my mind, at different times, that I was under the influence of the devil. This fear was a great mercy of God, for had his Spirit ceased to strive with me, I should have rested content on the brink of ruin, and have fallen a victim, at last, to this device of the enemy of mankind. But blessed be God, he had not sworn yet that 1 should not enter into his rest. He spared me yet another year, while he digged about me, that, if possible, 1 should bring forth fruit. One day, 1 was at my class leader's house, and finding a number of the Methodist Magazine on the table, I took it up, and looking over the contents on the title page, I found there was a piece in, on the " Baptist's message to Christ." I felt curious to know what there was about it, and when I had read it, I was filled with shame and confusion, that a question so easily answered, should have been the means, in the devil's hands, to draw me away from the fountain of living water, and cause me to hew out to myself broken cisterns that could hold no water.

The statement in the Magazine, on the Baptist's message, shewed that the doubts on John's mind, might arise from Christ not working a miracle to release him from prison, and that we might as well wonder at the denial of Peter, the treachery of Judas, and the littleness of faith in the rest of the apostles, when they forsook him and fled, as wonder at the doubts that arose in the mind of the Baptist. This convinced me of the folly and madness of condemning the whole Christian system, because John was perhaps doubting; in this way of judging, 1 saw that the Old Testament might be proved to be a fable; for Moses, in the time of disappointment, had as little faith in God, and less than

John himself; for though God promised to him, when he first sent him to Pharaoh, that he would be with him, and, for the strengthening of his faith, enabled him to work miracles, and, that he might not expect success at once, foretold him that the king of Egypt would not let the Jews go, even by a mighty hand; yet when he did not succeed in his first message to Pharaoh, he complained as though he believed God was not able to make him successful, and to deliver his people. "Lord," said he, "wherefore hast thou so evil entreated this people? Why is it that thou hast sent me? For since I came to Pharaoh to speak in thy name, he hath done evil to this people, neither hast thou delivered thy people at all. Nor was Aaron's faith stronger, when he made the golden calf, built an altar before it, and proclaimed a feast to Jehovah. These recollections were particularly relieving to my mind, for 1 thought, if the want of faith in Moses and Aaron was no proof against the authenticity of the Old Testament, why should 1 doubt the truth of the New Testament, for the supposed want of faith in John? Why should 1 imagine a vain thing against the Lord's Anointed? 1 would rather that 1 had never known his goodness, than after 1 had known it, thus shamefully and wilfully to abuse it: O wretched man that 1 am, who shall deliver me from the body of this death? Such reflections as these crowded my mind. As 1 walked homeward, amid awful thunder and lightning, 1 fancied every thing that came in my view reproached me, and to heaven 1 dared not to lift my eyes, for fear the clouds would burst on my head. When 1 came home, I hastened to my chamber to humble myself on my knees before God, and though 1 felt most wretched, and had no hopes of enjoying the favour of God, yet 1 felt thankful that my eyes were open, as it gave me an opportunity of owning my wickedness before him. 1 was in this miserable state of mind for some time, and my prayers consisted of nothing but confessions of my guilt. I durst not ask for pardon, nor could 1 plead the blood of the Saviour, after trampling it as it were under foot, and calling it an unholy thing.

Some weeks after this, my master was reading to us on a Sunday night, a section in Doddrige's Rise and Progress, instead of a sermon as usual. In order to make some part of it plain, he introduced the extraordinary conversion of Colonel Gardiner, and when he described the vision of the cross the Colonel saw, I felt my blood run cold within my veins, a shivering came over me, and 1 trembled lest 1 should see the Saviour bearing his wounds, and saying, " Why persecutest thou me?" Oh! it was hard for me "to kick against the pricks." 1 could not help picturing to myself in my heart, the affecting scene on Calvary; but when 1 saw the nails in my Saviour's hands and feet, and the blood streaming from his side, instead of being reproached as 1 feared, the words came to my mind, "1 suffer this for you." 1 began to hope, but not without fear, that the day of salvation was nigh. On Monday, the family was from home, and while 1 was reading the 18th and 19th of St. John, 1 was greatly affected, and felt disposed to pray. 1 hastened to a room by myself, and, while 1 there pleaded the Saviour's merits, I began to feel my strength renewed, and as though God said to me " be it according to thy word, go in peace, and sin no more." Thus I was once more enabled to rejoice in the boundless love of the Redeemer, and pour out my gratitude to him, who had so wonderfully delivered me out of the paws of the lion. Now I could sing

> Yes, the lion is once more
>   Defrauded of his prey,
> Though he thrust at me full sore,
>   I am not fall'n away;
> Satan long'd my soul to seize,
>   Like wheat t' have sifted me;
> Jesus pray'd, and kept me his,
>   And his I still shall be.

When 1 had lived in this family nearly two years, having written several times to my relations in Poland, without receiving any answer to my letters, 1 felt great uneasiness in my mind; and fearing I should never be fully settled, until 1 knew whether "my old father was yet alive," and what had become of my mother and her children, 1 resolved to leave my situation, and by the first opportunity that should offer, return home for a short time. When 1 acquainted my master with this intention, he was grieved at my imprudence: and though he did his best to dissuade me from a step which he feared would be ruinous both to my temporal and spiritual state, yet 1 found the temptation unconquerable, and gave him to understand that 1 would leave my place when the two years were completed. On the

13th of July, 1830, 1 left the family, and my master gave me a good character, and I had the good wishes of all around me. It was not, however, without much regret that 1 left them, as I was satisfied in my mind that 1 could not get a better situation of the kind.

When 1 came to Liverpool, my former friends were quite astonished at the whims 1 had taken into my head, and not one of them approved of my intention, and so much did they speak against it, that I was resolved not to go, unless I should perceive providence in my favour. 1 began to look out for a situation, either as footman in a gentleman's family, or as steward in a ship, resolving to accept of the one that would turn up first. 1 heard first of a steward's place, on board a vessel which was bound for Quebec. 1 engaged to go for two pounds ten shillings a month. On the day, however, that she was expected to sail, the owners changed her destination, and instead of going to Quebec, we sailed, on the first of August, for the Baltic, 1 thought fortune was favouring me, as this voyage would bring me near my home, but clouds will arise sometimes though the day promises fair. 1 was rather unwell when we left Liverpool, and in consequence of sea sickness, 1 became very ill, and could scarcely attend to my duty. This was very trying to me, as the captain, though a good man, often believed the tales of the crew, that my illness was a mere pretence, and thus 1 suffered persecution from all around me. We had contrary winds, and very stormy weather, and were a month in sailing to Elsinore. By the time, we arrived here, illness had reduced me to such a degree, that 1 could scarcely walk about the deck, and 1 plainly saw that 1 should be of no service to the ship, and that remaining among these persecuting sailors might prove my death, so 1 solicited the captain to put me ashore at Elsinore. This he refused to do, as the law required him to bear my expences until 1 recovered; but after we had set sail again, on my promising to sign a certificate that 1 would make no claim on the captain, ship, or owners, he consented to let me go. In order that 1 might have as much money with me as possible, 1 sold all my new clothes under value, and then 1 went on shore with the pilot that took us through the Elsinore grounds, to a place called Dracow, about twenty-four miles from Elsinore, whence we had to proceed back to that town by land, through Copenhagen. We travelled in a very uncomfortable cart, and 1 thought 1 should be shaken to pieces before we arrived at the end of our journey. About twelve at night, we rested at an inn, eight miles from Elsinore, in order to give the horses some fodder. Here we found some company drinking, and the pilot joined with them in conversation, and though 1 could not understand them, yet 1 perceived it was a dispute. After some time, the pilot addressed himself to me, saying "now you are an Englishman, can you tell me if we cease to exist, when we die." Having expressed my wonder that they who professed to be Christians, should be so ignorant, 1 answered, " when we die, we go to live in another world, either in happiness or misery, according to our character." When the pilot told the rest of the company my opinion, they wished him to ask me "whether any one came down from heaven, or up from the grave to assure us of this." "I have only professed Christianity a short time," said 1, "for I was born a Jew; yet I have had plenty of time to find out who came down from heaven, and up from the grave; and it is strange that you who have professed Christianity all your lives, should not know it. Did not Christ come down from heaven, and did he not, after death, rise from the grave? He has brought immortality to light." They all cried out "*pravou*" or bravely said, and asked me to take a glass. We now proceeded on our journey, and 1 was very glad when we arrived at Elsinore, and lodged with the pilot, who treated me very kindly. 1 was several weeks before 1 recovered my strength sufficiently to walk about, during which time, 1 had spent the little money I had brought with me, and 1 began to be in want. The winter also had set in, and the doctor whose advice I took, advised me not to venture out to sea. The war had also broken out in Poland, and prevented my proceeding home, and what to begin at in this foreign land, I did not know. I made, however, my wants known to that God who said, "call upon me in the day of trouble, and 1 will hear thee, and thou shalt glorify me." When I informed the pilot that 1 understood the duties of a footman, he observed that there had lately come a new British consul to Elsinore, and that he was in want of a servant, and if 1 liked he would introduce me to him. We went together, and the pilot recommended me to him, and related my sorrowful tale. Mr. M'Gregor expressed sorrow that I had not called sooner, for he said, I engaged a man only two days ago. We then called on Mr. Fenwick, the former consul's son, who said, I wish I had seen you yesterday, I might have recommended you to the American consul at Copenhagen, but he got suited last night. We now met the brother of the captain of the guard ship, to whom the pilot related my misfortunes. He said he was sure his brother was in want of a man, and that if I would wait at the quay, he would see him, and let me know the result. He returned in a quarter of an hour, and was very sorry to say, that his brother gave his word to a man only an hour ago. I could not help now beginning to shed tears at the seeming frownings of Providence, thinking all these things were against me.

Seeing I had no prospect of earning my bread, I resolved to return to Liverpool by the first vessel that would take me, in spite of the doctor's advice. With this determination, I walked out to the quay along with the pilot. In going, we met an old gentleman, and the pilot said, this is Mr. Chapman, senior, I think you had better ask him whether he wants a servant. As the pilot had taken a great deal of trouble with me, I could not refuse to take his advice, so I went up to Mr. Chapman, and made my request known to him, when he replied, "just come into the office, and I will hear you." After I had given him answers to several questions, and shewn him my certificates, he said he should be in want of a footman in about a week, as his old servant was intending soon to be married, and if I thought 1 could undertake the situation, he would engage me. We immediately agreed, and he sent for a tailor, and ordered my livery. He also paid the pilot all I owed him, and my expenses during the week 1 had got to stay with him. In this respectable family, 1 lived six months as comfortably as I could expect, considering 1 was surrounded by Danish servants, with whom 1 could converse very little, and had no opportunity of joining in public worship, as it was all performed in Danish. Through this latter privation, 1 did not continue with them. I left them on the 12th of May, 1831, with a good character, and the hearty good wishes of all around me. My old acquaintance, the pilot, recommended me to captain Greenwool, who commanded a Prussian bark, called the Idona of Dantzic, who promised to give me my passage, if 1 would work for it. 1 agreed with him, and we set sail for Liverpool, on the 15th of May. We had a tolerable voyage, and arrived at Liverpool about the middle of June. I was treated well by all the crew, and the captain expressed his satisfaction, by making me a handsome present, on our arrival. 1 was truly thankful to the God of Providence, that 1 had my feet once more on the British shore, where, in years that were past, 1 had received so many instances of the Divine care. I hastened to visit my old friends, who all welcomed the prodigal home from the far country, and, while 1 related to them news from abroad, they informed me of what had passed at home. With other things, they told me that there was now open a place in Liverpool, for the conversion of the Jews, called the Hebrew Church, for Christian Israelites, and that the Rev. H. S. Joseph, a converted Jew, was the minister over it, and that he was a means of doing much good. 1 rejoiced to hear this, and felt happy to think that God was about to have mercy on the outcasts of Israel. I could not help feeling a wish that 1 had some active part in this service, though it were but a door-keeper's. The first opportunity 1 had, I went to see this Jewish convert, and, to my great astonishment and rejoicing, 1 recognized him as the person whom 1 had once known as the Jewish rabbi at Bedford. We were very glad to see one another, and particularly to see one another as Christians. Some days after this, Mr. Joseph had occasion to dismiss his clerk, and he offered to take me in his place. The salary was £20. a year, which I expected would make me comfortable, if I could also follow a little business during the week. Some of my friends would not advise me to engage, but others did; and, as I had a great wish from the beginning to have some employment in this church, 1 took the advice of the latter. The congregation seemed well satisfied with my performances, and I liked the duty very well; but as the lady who patronized the church, paid but little of my salary, and that little in such trifling sums as did me not much good, 1 was obliged to think of giving up my office. 1 so-

licited some of my friends to procure for me a footman's place, which they did not find soon enough to
keep me from want; and rather than suffer longer, 1
purposed going to sea. 1 knew my friends would not
approve of it, and 1 thought of going to the sailors'
register office, and get a ship without troubling them.
At the office, however, 1 must pay 1s. 6d. upon being
registered, of which sum, I was not in possession, and
I could not for shame inform my friends of this want,
When going about the dock one morning wrapped in
meditation, 1 saw a gentleman who, 1 fancied, was
brother to Mrs. Lace, walking within the Goree Pi-
azzas. He recognized me, and asked me various
questions about my welfare, and though 1 gave him
no immediate explanation, yet he put his hand into
his pocket and took out two shillings, which he gave
me, saying, "This is all 1 have in my pocket," and
away he went. 1 was astonished that I had not presence of mind to inquire after the health of the family,
or to thank him for his kindness, which may God reward. 1 tried my best, but I could not get to see him
again. Having thanked the gracious Providence of
God, I hastened to the register office, and got booked,
and the next day, 1 was engaged as steward to a vessel
bound for Sierra Leone.

My friends were all very sorry at my new adventure,
and though they spoke of the unhealthiness of the cli-
mate 1 was bound to, and the difficulties of a long
voyage, 1 was still resolved, as the motive of my going
was the earning of my bread, and the improving of

my circumstances; and 1 hoped that the Saviour and Guardian of my soul would cause all these things to work together for my good. 1 joined the ship on the 28th of October, 1831, and we arrived all safe at our destined haven on the last of December. Here we remained all in good health, (except an old man, who was ill when we left Liverpool, and who died on our passage home,) until the middle of April, 1832, when we with great joy weighed anchor, and set 'sail for Liverpool. We were two months on our passage, and in the middle of June we happily arrived at the Queen's Dock. During this time I endeavoured to meet the trials common to long voyages, while surrounded by an irreligious crew, with Christian fortitude. The captain, though not a professor of religion, treated me with great kindness; and though I innocently got into trouble through him at Liverpool, respecting some contraband goods, from which 1 was honourably acquitted by the Board of Customs, yet 1 must own that during the time of my sufferings, he behaved very well to me. However, 1 took the advice of my friends, not to expose myself to the dangers and temptations of a seafaring life, if 1 could possibly avoid it. And thus when I had settled with my kind captain, and returned thanks to the great Disposer of all events for his past goodness, 1 resolved to try some way of getting a living without having occasion to wander from the land flowing with milk and honey.

As 1 could not meet with a situation that appeared at all likely to be comfortable and permanent, with the

advice of some of my friends, 1 chose, in order to obtain a livelihood, to travel with stationery and other
articles, at the same time purposing to carry the best
goods, to take a reasonable profit, and to make only
one price. But 1 am sorry to say, that the trials 1 have
met with in this undertaking, have been far beyond what
I could have anticipated; for not only do I find myself
disowned by my relations, and treated unkindly by my
Jewish brethren at large,* but am even uncharitably
suspected by Christians, though 1 carry with me tes-
timonials of my character from persons of note, who
have known me ever since my conversion. From their
suspicions 1 have endured many trials, and many 1 do
still endure, which can only be felt by persons in simi-
lar circumstances. 1 will not, however enlarge on
these, for my hope is not in man, but in God alone,
who sees my heart. He has guided from my youth,
and has protected me until now: He will be my coun-
sellor unto death, and my eternal home. And 1 have
only referred to my difficulties that Christians may have
some view of what many Jews have to suffer when they
enlist under the banner of Christ, and that they may
be induced to remember them at the throne of grace.

1 must however acknowledge, as my readers have
already seen, that those Christians who have known

* The rabbies have a law that all Jews who embrace Christianity
should be treated with the utmost contempt, and that their names
should never be mentioned without saying, "*Yemach shemow
vizichrow*," viz. may his name and remembrance be blotted out.
The common name they give to a Jewish Christian is "*Meshomet*,"
which word signifies, not only an apostate, but one who is destroyed
or killed.

me, have sympathized with me in the day of trouble, and have afforded me suitable help. Without their kind attention, I must certainly have perished, or I must have apostatized from the Christian faith. To them I can only express my sincere thanks, and my hopes and prayers, that He who promised to reward even a cup of cold water given to his followers, may reward their kindness both in time and eternity.

And now, on looking back to the time when I embraced the Saviour of the world, I see great cause to humble myself before God, that notwithstanding the care he has taken of me, and the mighty deliverances he has wrought for me, I have often grieved his Holy Spirit, and have come far short of my duty. It is through the grace of God that I am what I am. " If it had not been the Lord who was on my side, then the waters had overwhelmed me, the billows had gone over my soul. Blessed be the Lord, who hath not given me a prey to the devourer, and who has enabled me to escape as a bird out of the snare of the fowler !"

> O to grace how great a debtor
> Daily I'm constrained to be !

May the Lord help me to shew forth to the world, by the remainder of my life, that I am a true disciple of Jesus Christ, and that I am saved by his atoning and all-cleansing blood ! I beg an interest in the prayers of the Christian reader, that God would keep me unmoveable in his service, and help me to hold fast my confidence steadfast unto the end.

THE

Christian's Prayer for the Jews.

Father of faithful Abraham, hear
  Our earnest suit for Abraham's seed!
Justly they claim the softest pray'r
  From us adopted in their stead,
Who mercy thro' their fall obtain,
And Christ, by their rejection, gain.

Outcasts from thee, and scatter'd wide,
  Through every nation under heav'n,
Blaspheming whom they crucified,
  Unsav'd, unpity'd, unforgiv'n;
Branded like Cain, they bear their load,
Abhorr'd of men, and curs'd of God.

But hast thou finally forsook,
  For ever cast thine own away?
Wilt thou not bid the murderers look
  On him they pierc'd, and weep, and pray?
Yes, gracious Lord, thy word is past,
All Israel shall be saved at last.

Come, then, thou great Deliverer, come!
  The veil from Jacob's heart remove;
Receive thy ancient people home!
  That, quicken'd by thy dying love,
The world may their reception find,
Life from the dead for all mankind.

H. WARDMAN, PRINTER, BRADFORD.

www.ingramcontent.com/pod-product-compliance
Lightning Source LLC
Chambersburg PA
CBHW081520040426
42447CB00013B/3287